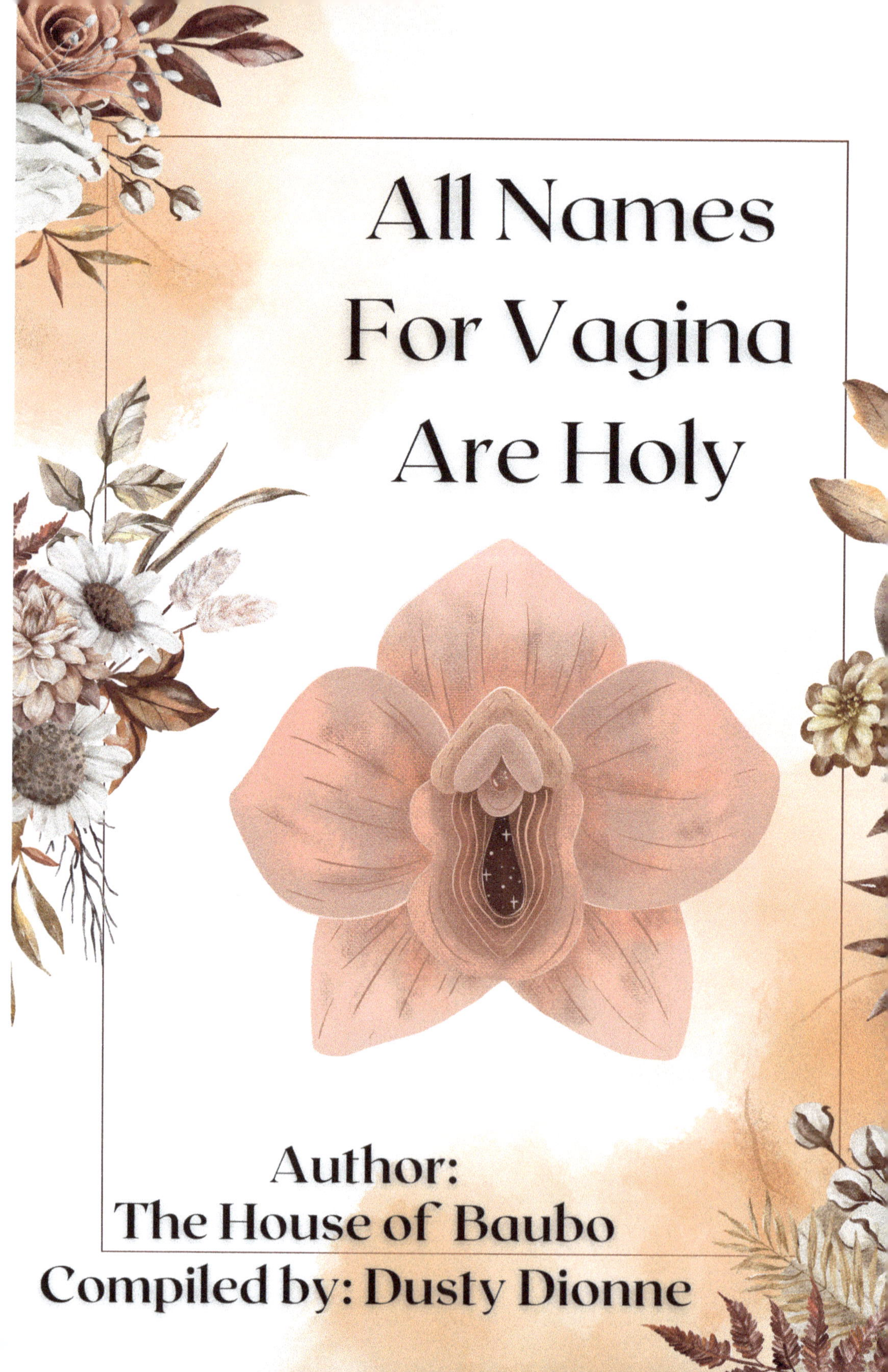

All Names
For Vagina
Are Holy
Author:
The House of Baubo
Compiled by: Dusty Dionne

Orphic Fragment 52
Baubo and Demeter

"This said, Baubo drew
aside her robes, and showed
A sight of shame; child
Iacchus was there,
And laughing, plunged her
hand below her breasts.
Then smiled the goddess, in
her heart she smiled,
And drank the draught
from out that glancing cup"

Coochie

CLAM

Sausage
Wallet

Clunge

Ax Wound

FLOWER

Twat

NOTES :

Mon2

HOLE

VAG

VAGOO

HOO-HOO

Turgid

WANG
ENFOLDER

There is no need
to rush.

FURBURGER

Cave of wonders

Kitty

HONEY POT

BAJINGO

Lady Bits

PINK
TACO

MEAT
CURTAINS

Foof

Something special is coming...

Beaver

LABIA MAJORIS

BOOK NOW

MON 14 PUSSY

TUE 15 PUSSY

WED 16 PUSSY

THU 17 PUSSY

MOSSY

CLEFT

INTRODUCING
POON
That's Right!

Downtown Bonanza

Cunt

VA-
jay-jay

A WIZARDS SLEEVE

Love Tunnel
Love Tunnel
Love Tunnel
Love Tunnel
Love Tunnel
Love Tunnel
Love Tunnel

Hair
Pie

FLANGE

Nether Regions

Calling all knights and princesses as we celebrate:
FRONT BUTT

FANNY

PEACHES & CREAM

A new sermon series

GASH

VERTICAL SMILE

SQUEEZE
BOX

"
PUSS-PUSS

LALA

BEARDED

BEAUTY

POON-TANG

Panty

Hamster

Red Wagon

Upright
Wink

GARAGE

Fish Lips

love button

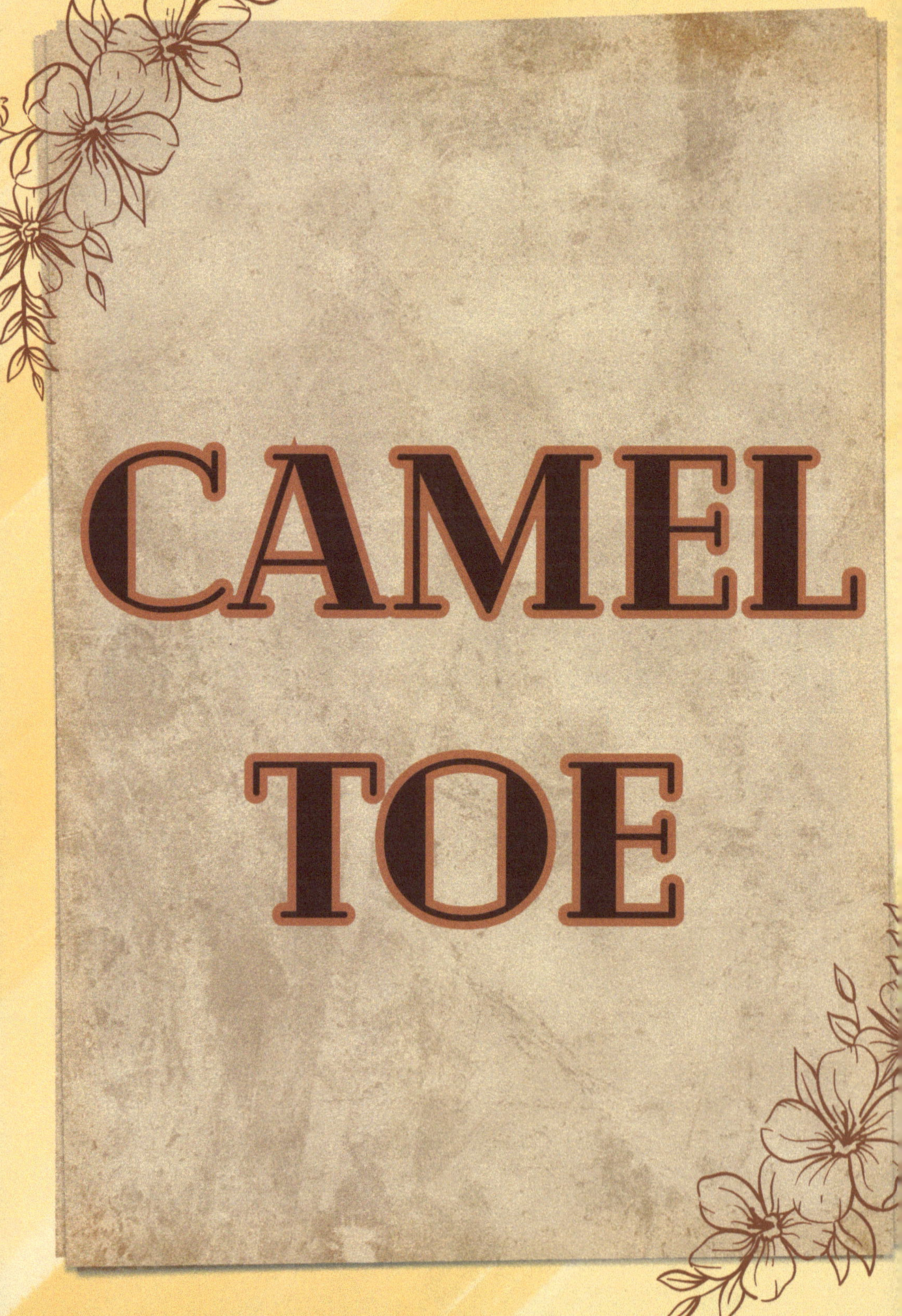

CAMEL
TOE

PI
Canoe
NK

Hippos
Yawn

Handwarmer

FLAPS

LIPS

SNATCH

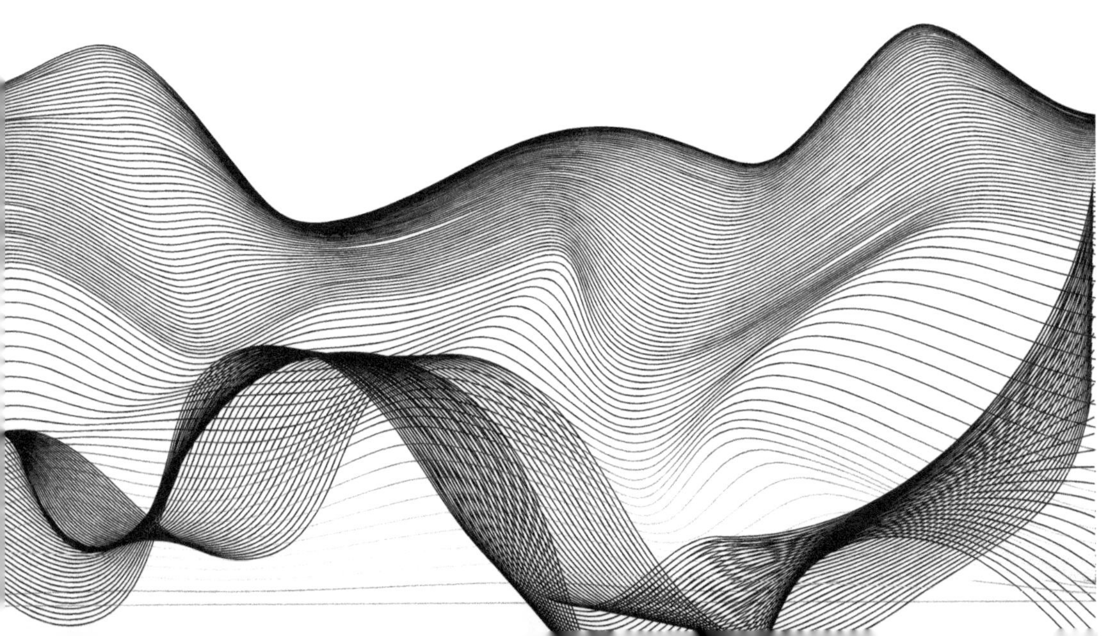

MONEY BOX

Purse

Notes
Quim

Minnie

popkin

CROTCH

Wonder Down Under

*Cum
Dumpster

Paris
Glove

Poonanny

PALOMITA

Moo-Moo

Schmoo

CRACK

VISUAL ART

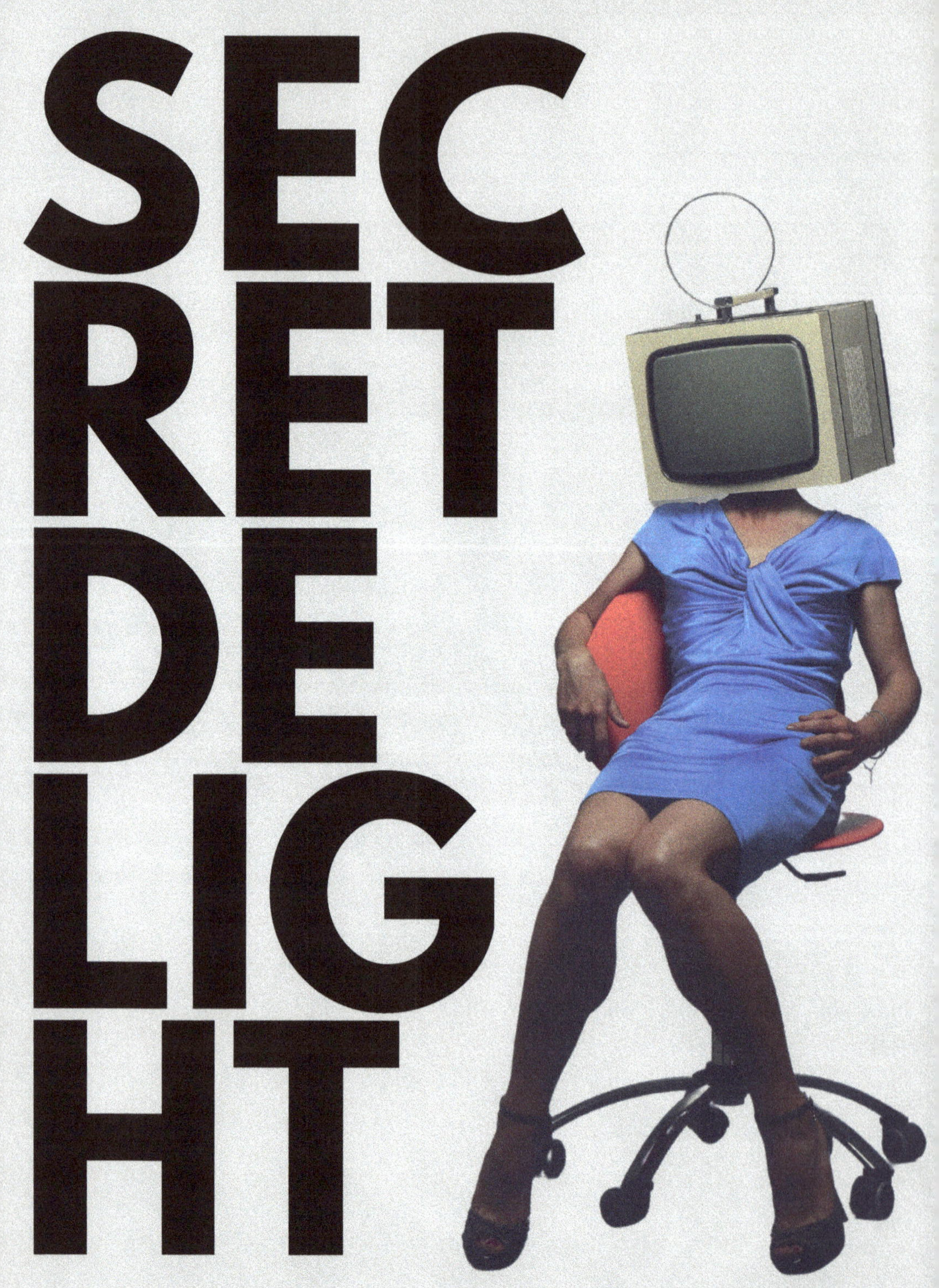

SEC
RET
DE
LIG
HT

Bush

COOTER

Coin Slot

Grand Opening

FRESH
FLOWER
MARKET

SHEATH

BLOOM

Squish Mitten

WHISKER
BISCUIT

CHEERS TO
SUGAR WALLS

Juice Box

Vuhjeen

Tuppence

pum · pum

n.

the maintaining of someone or something in life
or existence, regarding nourishment

MUMU
BUTTON

Weapon of love

Cherri Koko

Heaven

Fountain of
Pleasure

Promised Land

Yoni

Bikini

Biscuit

THIS MONTH'S FAVORITES

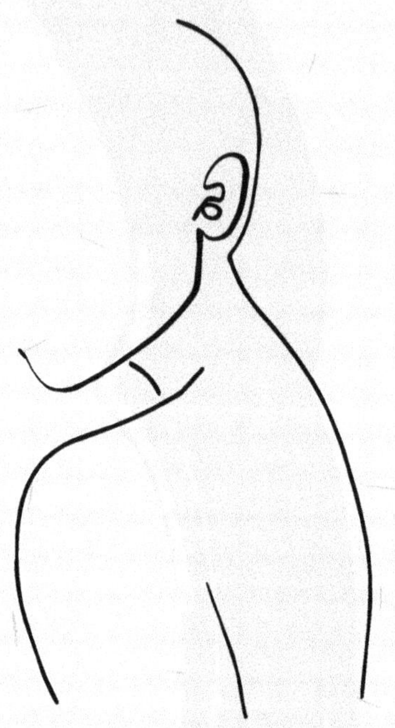

Snake Charmer

Hairy
Manilow

Tinkle
Flower

V.

A.

G.

I.

N.

A.